OVERWINTER

OVERWINTER

Jeremy Pataky

UNIVERSITY OF ALASKA PRESS   FAIRBANKS

University of Alaska Press
P.O. Box 756240
Fairbanks, AK 99775-6240

ISBN 978-1-60223-253-2 (paperback); ISBN 978-1-60223-254-9
(electronic)

Library of Congress Cataloging-in-Publication Data
Pataky, Jeremy.
  [Poems. Selections]
  Overwinter / Jeremy Pataky.
    pages cm
  ISBN 978-1-60223-253-2 (pbk. : alk. paper)—ISBN 978-1-60223-
254-9 (electronic)
  I. Title.   PS3616.A86644A6 2015   811'.6—dc23
                        2014023211

Cover design by Kristina Kachele
Interior design by Taya Kitaysky
Cover image by Eamon Mac Mahon (aerial photograph of the
Taku Glacier near Juneau)

This publication was printed on acid-free paper that meets the
minimum requirements for ANSI / NISO Z39.48–1992 (R2002)
(Permanence of Paper for Printed Library Materials).

CONTENTS

III.

IV.

V.

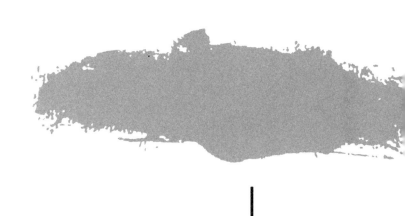

FIVE PARTS

The land is made from five parts: shelter,
mountain, ground, and lake. — Nigel Peake

Shelters here
are nothing like barns
nothing like stone huts.

The land is made of glacial flour
and fossilized rivers. The shelters
dissolve back into ground.

Mountains deliver water to the lake.
The lake is new. It shrinks and grows.
The life is made from five parts:
shelter, mountain, ground, lake,

and ash. Shelter, mountain, ground, lake
and lack. The trees don't line up,
the river braids tangle and untangle.

Structures of shelter, here,
don't last, are forest
and creek bed, are gone.

Are old foundations, former bridges
hollowed into ground.

The structures that are shelters, now,
are warmed by fires fed
with wood reclaimed from piles
of structures that have fallen.

Structures of shelter, here,
are drums for rain
played to an audience within.

MANUAL LABOR IN THE ERA OF DELINQUENT WEATHER

We arrived without boats
by way of the ramped-up violence
of a road's frost heaves,
the dilemma of organizing

a road's river stones in low winter water.
We filled the open space
with rescued cables and timbers
before activating through networks of chain letters.

The inferno embers resuscitate.
The cavern we carve is the cavity
aching up into a yardage of spruce smoke,
sudden scratch of a felt pen, a woman behind sunglasses
calling yellow-rumped warblers in
through poplars.

And if the river began
to gnaw out of its habits,
if it threatens the foundation
of the homemade bridge,
could stacking stones one at a time
have convinced it otherwise?
We put forth our sweat faith
and will accept the inundation to come.

WE WERE EXPLORERS ONCE

Ice breaks up each spring—
the ocean and rivers grow teeth

and lose them, place them
under pillows of fog

lose them to drifts of warmth
in the coldest, killingest depths

where small, edible whales
move like clots through a bloodstream,

where their shadows in the shallow seas
are vaguely alive, and vaguely something else,

the shape of old ships, the footprints of old explorers
tromping crabwise through some imagination.

To what end did we venture
out of the old world

to the endcaps of earth,
shelterless, wearing comely myths

we couldn't dream would become truths
up at the globe's neckline?

If our wants are trivial
our best wars are tussles,

our worst weather is rime on road signs,
breath off the water in the morning.

THEN TO NOW

You fret and wring each minute
into being, all cataloged
in long lists amid laughter
and phone-light, the rinds
of friends' aftersobs, their silent blessings.
You slim into a resemblance
of tunnels, tree bark,
last year's cranberries fermented
in the woods by the cemetery.

Are you the precise hour you think you are?
Do you squander the spoils of your prizefighting?

I regret nothing but encounters with you
because I left my last family members
for landscapes,
loneliness articulating a flock of waxwings
hungry for red, seedy berries.

Are you the gray world
or the red berries swallowed into birds?
Are you the stark branch
charming it on behalf of nighttime?

In this rebuilt warehouse storing historic dust
we ate the most recent meal in ten thousand meals.

Now the house is skewered by a stovepipe.
Now the blanched flowers fold every petal tight.
We battered dandelion heads, ate them.
Today a green inchworm, inching,
inched along my stitched arm.

REASONS FOR A LONG STAY

Know that others wrestle
with the truncation of the home's compass,
know they calibrate their compass needle
into the declinating metals
of one another, and be the reefs
of their could-be calamities, charted on
on a sheet of graph paper.
Tease sound out of a habit
of winter listening and
stroke a stuffed owl's beak.
Register the ascending synthesizer
of a Swainson's thrush and stay carelessly asleep.
To quiet down out on the deck, full night ablaze,
bulbous moon insignificant, drink
and speak to strangers. Imagine a cobweb
relating air temperature, flood threat,
distance from home, duration of camaraderie.
Deciding, derided, fall to sleep reading by handheld light.

ANTIDOTE

A creek cures quiet,
slurs out the unsounding day of pursed lips,
leads by example, barrels without straining,
stresses what sickens into it, slats the platted bluff,
wrests birches into itself,
rockfall clatter subliminal beneath,
birds calling out their spring needs.
Creek makes a good fence,
better than stone piles, centuries,
a field, bones of fish,
woodpiles, lichen one day
wrapping a cairn into place.
Silence at a creek is daylong,
days long, swollen and uncrossable.
A creek can make a good fence,
neighbor to nothing, grumbling
in darkness through which its erosion
and clatter is just audible,
trees toppling over the steep bluff, into water.
A creek thickened into one channel
tries to braid itself,
is a torrent that seeks to shallow and calm itself
beside me here, living, unfenced, the leaves
patching away the sky and weather,
the nature of this tin roof
amplifying rainfall

as leaves, grown just since middle May,
amplify winds and muddle the water's murmur.

WOOD HEAT

I come from those who trim unseemly branches,
who edit for horizons, lake views.

I climbed trees and cut them down,
got caught in their fine crooks dizzyingly high

then worked my way back to earth
and felled them for the fireplace.

The waver of opaque smoke coughed upward.
My grip has been sticky with pitch

like my calluses, my clothes.
From my grandfather's basement,

cement wood room
with a trapdoor to the outdoors,

a hydraulic log splitter, my own axe,
a pocket knife, the dog eyeing birds.

I'm my own axe, a woodpile.
Fires bundled, left on the stoop.

If one loves trees one almost loves
the self, also almost others?

We nailed birdhouses to trees
and watched birds through windows of our house.

We kept wooden matches at hand.
Fire was our crackling

iteration of a plan to go on
and on we meant to go.

RUNOFF

It's morning in the lower west
where you retreated and seasoned in.
And summer heat is a snow slope
where you dug out a hibernation cave,
you landscaped the arid valley
with the rivers passing through,
you drove treelineward with the sunroof
open to the first rain
as birds pummeled the voices of DJs—

drops leap but not free of the stream,
and I shed layers.
The sun grazes close and
ice is linoleum in the valley.

Water magnetized water
and the town held you and your orbit
became a ceremony of trying to go, waterborne,
on out, anonymous, common.
Leave the power lines and wires,
leave behind ditches aspiring onward.

Aspire, break free.
I was the only one going anywhere.
Gravel pelted the underbelly
of the vehicle. I squinted into brightness and
went out from there where you are.

11

A BRIEF HISTORY
OF LANDING HERE

All the phone calls clotted a hum in my inner ear.
And every walk became a thick pencil underlining the same

three newspaper sentences until the paper shredded.
Every vine-ripened song throbbed

into airspace toward fighters looking for you
deckside on your friendly aircraft carrier.

How enticing, the glance you flung
like a neighbor tossing a pail of water onto a house fire.

Signal the birds in then jump.
Twirl your orange sticks like sparklers or hurl them.

How enticing, your good harmonizing,
your tambourine jangling in the back of your rickety pickup—

turn off your turn signal and sing,
something like the note you left on the table,

take the alley home and park cockeyed on the yard
and know this: I am inside pitting your feral cherries.

I am forwarding each piece of your mail.

THE PARTICULARS OF
THE BUILT ENVIRONMENT

Jets descend past me
into a pastel town sky
and disappear as stones
sink into water. Mallards and teal settle
on the slush slough of a half-frozen river.
I remember your strangest idea,
the tune slip of your voice under nerves,
common hair growing from your body,
the yellow of grasses under melted snow.
I can guess your altitude,
the airplane window framing your dreams.
You're no given and I have belittled
the habit of correspondence with distant
friends who travel to relish
home water out of a tap.
There's a man in the village
watching the strip your plane will know
and he is the poisoner
of dogs, wolves.
Gaze fraught with gales,
he gillnets the swum awe
of our homing instincts,
dragnetting sea vents, the soft
tissues of your body
which are, I imagine,

the brightest aquatic creatures
inside the opaque gut
of the ocean.

COUNTING DOWN TO A DESTINATION WITHIN BLISS

This valley is a cusp of staying,
this river is bridged and the vertebrae
of the bridge forms a catwalk of metal.
We have more bridges than rivers
in this town of not-quite-giving-in.
This town of every time I try
I hear erosion,
town of the flood,
town without travel.
You can wear the rivers with your eyes,
look between your feet,
another reinhabited nest, a den,
a lodge, real estate, unreal.

BAROMETRIC PRESSURE

The rain makes
a child's broken xylophone
of the tin roof.

The cabin door is open
toward a mountain
obscured from view

by leaves and weather.
I sit with a photograph—
somewhere near the vanishing point

I see myself, exposed
by a horizon
that I sit on like a wall.

I picked sage in the sun
from the bluff by the river
while the engine idled—

it dries, hung in the cabin,
and the cabin smell
includes rain and coffee

but not sage.
Rain makes a motion-stop
sound collage of a campfire

burning bubble wrap.
If this cabin were your ear
I would whisper the names

of every road we drove
to get to the end
of the near-most road.

We wore raingear and rubber boots.
We were incensed with communal living.
We coveted favorite spoons.

The rain sings cat tongue licks of your memory.
The sound tastes me, rough and clean.
The river has swollen, and there's no way to know

which tree will fall off the far bluff next.
You leak into this moment
though you are near saltwater, the city,

are you this water emerging
from the rock levy, are you
the dry bed filling

with pieces of the gray river,
was I the sound of unseen boulders rolled
in the river's last flood?

HERE WE ARE

I listen to every voice I left to be here
repeating the last little words I heard.
I am a pathway out of them.
Why won't they write.
When was the last talk.
I am back in my body, nearly,
I am on the way here by a new magnetism
reminiscent of early, pre-industrial
gravity and cloud shadow,
pastoral landscapes uncanonized by oil.
We paint ourselves with silt mud
without decorum or devotion.
This fallout is a residue of sweat
and our curtains were torn down
and soaked in paint thinner.
We flip the calendar,
enamored with rain on the cabin window.
We may or may not be in this together.
We may or may not remember this tomorrow,
though the story will pass on and on and on.

FIRE IN THE SUCCESSION ZONES

A bee pollinates the fireweed's top blossom
untroubled by mirrors reflecting anything.
I reflect nothing but the light glinting from your skin.
And by the lagoon, in that sun, I could foresee
missing you, the day of the bakery and bicycles.
Your house in the city
sheds rain into streets, the streets
shed rain to sewers. The glaciers grew
from the talismans of their own
homemade clouds, and I live someplace
quietly and well, and the thought
of you is muffled by the hum of this creek
flowing endlessly and loud,
silty, then clear again, and small planes blaze by,
enough intrusion to hollow out this silence,
you are inside it,
you are inside this, aren't you,
aren't you the density of this burning forest's smoke—
the fire line singes the river.
You sweat but your feet are in cold water,
our bodies are in the noise of the river,
in the noise of burning, we're burning,
we're burning, you're burning this down.

FROM HERE YOU SEEM A BRAIDED RIVER

You wore shorefast ice,
birds were starting,
spring high water
was still white snow
in mountains.
Ice still rimmed your banks.
We would come to know gibbous light.
We would come to know snow light.
We would come to know ice light, star, animal
light, window light, want light,
sweat light. We'd know the light of the river rippling
shadows on the shadows. We'd know
candid light, we'd know dinner light and laughter light,
we'd know light off the underside of owl wings,
melt light and the light of the woods,
the light of letters, light of the dash
and the strange feathers of baleen on blank walls.
We'd know rain light and dream light. We'd know the peaceful
light of a single morning, we'd know the
thick light beneath the bridge. We'd know
the light of our clamor to belong in all light,
we'd know bluegrass light
and aquatic light, tundra light, intermountain light and
the light of surprise—

I know iceless light of you,
winter light, spring light, speech light of you,
light of seeing you, memory light,
photograph, ache light, light of one of these days,
light of so much left to say,
light of one day, light of one night
and one morning, light of one day.

SCREEN

In this private nighttime an ocean is behind us.
Between us and the ocean, deciduous trees bear leaves.

I have put on a necktie for you.
I dedicate this perfect double Windsor knot to you.

I am telling you this because of our devout blindness
which was your idea and now I understand why.

The fasting was a beginning and now it is
impossible to eat through a white cloth

draped over the face. Let us begin, this way, again—
save the absence of your scars.

We are projectionists of private myths.
This habit of looking beyond you when I speak to you.

AURAL

We were all on time, once
hunkered in the medians

attuned to the addled clamor
where we built our nests.

No need to make
attempts on some new world

no cause for forward thinking.
And if the sound of lifting jets

eclipses the false noise of traffic
give up all listening and let the sounds

hemorrhage into whatever memories
of natural quiet you can find,

unbidden as a memory of taste
or a scent wafting into a sleep

your first rain on your first roof
calling birds muted by the river in flood.

III

FATA MORGANA

Your hands plumb spring's chinook throat.
Weather, lour, atop faults holding breath
like a tremor, over you
the whole wracked firmament
a map of saccades,
your quick breath as the moist
rain seeps into clothing,
onto skin, tease of wind
updrafting beneath an umbrella,
scintillant citrus light
on the table by a wine refraction,
Spanish wine, light haphazard
on the tablecloth, cube of squash
on a white ceramic plate,
kernel of dried maize, shawl
around you, a wrap around your body,
wrapped within a prescience
of spasm, ache, swell, your closed-lip
smile in a wood-floored curio cabinet
bathed in a pale light limning surfaces
shaping the room and the used dishes
and the books, bones and bird eggs, vases,
a jar housing a scintilla of misgiving,
the world's most careful paper crane.

You tunesmith the residue of petrichor,
snowfall, your feet holing through,
humming your walk under thin trees,
skeletal. Translate the smell of cold,
smell wet snow, smell a warm house baking bread.

Your face hinges into stories, your hair
braided and mussed by wind
veils your sunglasses—

but an ache throbs
while your hearing shades into purples, tonics,
you buckle, the fraught distance distends—

My eyes on you try to be my eyes in you
looking down into
the hole in a desert floor—
I'm looking at you looking into your days,
a fiction, I know no particulars, can't breathe rain smell
the instant after rain begins, not there, not in your nostrils,
not in the desert you grew from, not at the reservation
burial ceremony, invisible
from transcontinental flights,
irrelevant to jets,
blind to the canyons slung lissome
and the mourners, you, I imagine,
clutching sand, clutching clay.

You described burying a friend in the ground, no coffin. All dead I've seen have been animal, nameless, on the road, on beaches, in boats, woods, dry rivers, some lapped onto rife stones of a small spawning lake, some I have dug holes for, a dog, a wounded rodent we placed next to a stick to measure its nocturnal efforts, some in pickup beds, or half-tarped on a flatbed trailer at a stoplight, antlered. A gecko under a boot heel at a Key Largo road stop. You described burying a friend, pouring turquoise and clay into the grave, the blanket slipping away from the face. Now I'm home, enisled, memory of the smell of dead salmon, their water bodies emitting an earthy stench. I found a dead eagle beside the ocean, talons medieval, clutching nothing but the far north's misleading light, the distended days, fraudulent mornings of winter, and ambling sunsets, an hour and a half of vivid, livid colors, and the fata morgana far down the inlet, the light aching out of the ground, the mountains growing visibly, and I left it, once. And now you describe burying a friend in the ground, a teenager, and I return to a book about Arctic exploration, tricks of light traveling through unevenly tempered air, whole islands perceived, navigated toward, mapped, fled from, sought out tens of years later, the same illusion, just light, one could sail a boat safely through it like a somnolent jet beveling out a cloud. And reading about the problem of looking ahead or behind oneself in the white Arctic, no contrast, white on white on white, then black, white, white, no contrast, no depth perception, no opportunity for comparisons—a distant polar bear, a nearby snowshoe hare.

You are sitting on a wooden bench,
leaning against a bakery, and I imagine you
pouring dry clay, turquoise granule
handfuls on his face, corn rain
on his teeth, tart blue-greens, umbers,
yellows, and handfuls of earth to fill his hole in sere desert,
hole of his mouth behind lips
not saying not ravel heat glint
off a silver bracelet sweating into your eyes
chthonic stench and slow stones
raining through tannic earth,
sidereal pebbles—
without contrast, no depth perception.
A large, distant animal is a small animal near,
and the small, actual animal nearby disappears
and materializes, goes again, feet away, gone, there.

Weathers glint off your fixed eyes,
and through those sheens of cloud and rain,
wind patterns in tall grass,
stain of wind spilling across a calm bay,
static of a frozen sea under aurora, your gaze
leaking some of your tenebrous interior,
leaking it, exchanging some of mine,
ingesting the night fluid.

In distance, you are lambent,
fata morgana serrating the horizon
into windswept arêtes
smudged in the bizarre clarity of a whiteout.

Two great and contrasted forms of ritual
weft your sylph silence inward—
You have suggested this to me, your eyes
against the curtains, a pencil in your hand.
I am telling your story and using your language
and the yard is a patchwork
of yellow, dry grass, and the room's accumulating flies,
smoke, the volume of the music grows louder,
the ceiling is a patchwork of shadow and still
you stay: we are looking for our names
markered onto dollar bills and thumbtacked to the ceiling—
we have pressed our fingers into the grillwork of our eyes—

On the trail, the great horned owl flew over me, gently, close enough for its sound, arc down, extrapolated rise and light. Your father walked back down the trail fifty feet, looked, found the bird watching us, whistled, hooted, it turned its head. You and your mother down the hill, in trees, prostrate in shade and sun, dappled. Windswept cloud prints across the meadow, the sounds of birds and insects around us and seeping in us, the dry grass, dry dirt, shifting light. That owl, your birth, an owl atop your house, your plans for such birds, and stories of birds and dead boys, all of those herons, they're a-wing and they are painted, it's a simultaneity, they all have you in common, and the problem of borrowing what isn't mine and trying to make something of it, your eyes on your story that isn't yours, your face reflected, distorted, in the grimed chrome of a rented automobile's hubcap. You understand even as the isosceles swing set transforms into a broken mobile and the yard becomes your crib. What part of the story could possibly last? How much will we attribute to syntax? How can a mouth full of dirt speak in music? Was the imperative ever urgent? Tell me how to go about getting on, carrying you, glutting the haphazard forsythia on the barest, most essential sunlight, form something and fire it in a kiln fueled with cigar boxes and ponderosa pine cones, glaze up the prehistory under a salt sheen keening the song of a restless strait.

If weather goes against you do you give in to it?

Our long season ossified the light—

What shelf for the hand-tied flies
        made with mallard feathers

Where in the light to glint
        sun off their iridescent side-stripes?

Tell me the dead don't need names,
sky about to split, death-mask of a boy,
clay in your palms, some sweat.
Tell me I can hear your stories, write them.
I inhabit a room where I remember you
and I've seen you pause, look,
valence of a jukebox crocus abloom,
its yellow rivets in the spring of last call,
its disaster plans, its floodplains and fire routes,
the siren sidelining, the skatepark mess of adolescents,
the meals, the geese and mallards, the osprey
circling us, their nest, the water hazing off the bathroom
mirror where I showered. You say the word *tomorrow*,
finishing a sentence, and twist the key
you've inserted into your bicycle lock.

A baguette, a bridge, the salt scent of ocean,
the silence of otters, of seals, we were—are—on the ocean,
enisled, moony, similar, you luminesced
bringing tidings of riptide whale tremor, krill-thick
baleen licks, the very moon summiting
our private mountain, its tree line,
and I borrow your story because
you, yourself, with friends, with the family, buried
a boy, a body, wrapped in a blanket come slight off his face, buried
a deceased friend with your hands, your friends, the material
you put there, your fingers, your
fingers, my fingers,
my two windows admitting light,
your eyes, my fingers, my hand,
my fingers, your back, your scalp, your arms,
your hand, your fingers,
your knees, my room, your calves, your ankles,
feet, my hands, your feet, toes, your hair
(a strand the next day), your face, your face, your forehead,
your ears, your arms, your face, your eyes, your neck,
your throat, my blankets, my music, my place, my voice, your back,
your lowlight luminescing
through the thought sheen of your attention to the world,
your voice for addressing domestic cats, your back,
every mode parceled into you, I parse the impact
of your collapses, I am getting at a vision
of you, I tell the story to myself
regarding your funeral position, your fingers releasing material,

your hand with its three shadows, later, without me,
resting against bare paper,
its pen, you have buried the corpse
of a beloved with fists of sand, dirt, turquoise and I call it
bone rain? Or stars? Him a firmament, and I carry a scent,
a touch, and vision, watching, want,
confluence of what it is that we seem grateful to have?

I don't smell the desert or drench
in the drift of undocked creosote.
I don't beseech an answer, a treaty,
an optimism from the wrought
honky-tonk tremble,
prescription of notebook
playlist, your four-door still dependable, your steering
wheel I've handled from here to way off.
You've made no mistake about the stories. And I've listened
and written in margins, a phone number on the inside cover—
your phone, found, your money, found, your self, recovered.
You're walking neighborhoods and who knows
your hands have spilled earth onto the body of a boy, deadened.
The worlds you temper into this world, the smile you eye off my way.
Unacknowledged lives of birds come and go
three hundred feet above the unwatered lawn, the roof pitch,
the copper rooster turning on its axis with the canyon wind
while you do who knows what behind a door, ajar.

Above ground your sunroom, your enclosed patio, your miniature porch, your not-deck, not-room near your not-kitchen, its dwarf-everything, the pipe protruding, blunted, dead-end, from the wall, the vessels you made of clay. Above the street, that room built for weather viewing, weather against the windows as good as your body, which you windowed one night, unwittingly, while I dropped your neighbor off across the street. You windowed your body toward the darkness, from the kitchen, through the sunroom as I was pulling away from a full stop in the street, your entire building luminous, possibly actual against the vague darkness, a yellow arctic of light, fata morgana inked onto an artifactual map, all beneath sidereal habits, the firmament occulted by a proximal accident, the patterns we haphazard onto how we find our way under the mirage of relative movement, what backspots look like eyes to passing birds of prey, what wing feathers, tied, seem prey to fish, what ache or tremulous want supernovas in the chill interior winnowing there in the rooms where you so precisely dwell inside a lack of perceivable depth, ice blindness, dark, light's velocity through air and through water, too little contrast, too much, what isn't there that is and always was.

IV

SURVEYING

You shrink into your shut lids
and ask yourself which disaster to enact,

which persona to mimic like a plucked moth
wishing its way pupaward.

Wherever you sicken
into afternoons gone hot or swooning,

gone sweaty under bedcovers,
you elicit a lax wind from trees.

You speculate during the perusal
of a timbered property,

its intimate soil, the backyard
plot already rising—

wine with a dinner of mussels,
wine with cold light

filtered out of a dead latitude,
old windows framed up

by rough-cut lumber and the hard clamor of trains.
What home signals its small spore

into a trustworthy wind?
Your voice, ripe,

adorned with seeds.
Your ideas root

in a phalanx of trees
and in sunlight fading an old billboard.

Waiting ravishes
enflamed bodies.

Later by hours
you hatch from a cocoon.

You pick the berries and eat, eyeing
shapes the sky assumes around branches.

CONTEMPLATION, COMPOSITION, INTERPRETATION

The ground floor of the flooded hospital
is filled with creek rock.
From an eave one bird makes something
of the post-flood quiet,
fluting notes into wayward air,
safe travel, intransigence, a moment bandied out to hours.
To embark upon a continental migration
without our familiar heft
while expectations dissolve
and men commute with no
awareness of the cumulative power
of their respective commutes, the days blocked up with hours.
Geographic terms vary from region to region—
is the creek a river, canal a sound, the hill mountainous?
I hear the baroque theme of a film
ruined on a piano, better there
than on any harpsichord.

MODERNITY

The wood is as kind as moss,
as mushrooms colonizing
the hollow of a log,

and growth rings cram together,
erasing lives backward,
aging us toward youth.

The inmost sapwood
boils in the body, flesh,
in blankets, indoors.

I glimpsed her insides
during a laugh,
saw her softening core,

the muddy bottom
her keel dragged
dodging rocks

and the bones of sunken whales
with starfish sockets,
seaweed raiment.

Beneath her unsunned
winter skin colored
with light leached

from heartwood,
her tick-tocking little
factory went slowly to the birds

and the mold
and the rotting memories
of old-timers who grew up

working their inmost
with coarse and gentle hands.

HOW THE MISTRESS, DISTRESSED, INSINUATED HERSELF INTO PLACE

It's worth noting that you saw nothing
and I blame my silence on the smoke of the forest
burning beyond the river, threatening,
I blame the sex on the risk
of fire jumping the river, on your long drive
into the inside of something vast
yet unmapped, something once
fixed in place,
a blueprint kind of place,
but here, you escape, reject, even, not just
topo maps but topography itself.
Could you have broken me in?
Yes, that shape is the rotting terminus of an old, long glacier.
Yes, there are mountains out there someplace
and I saw them yesterday and for years before
you showed up and I'll see them when you go.
Yes, I understand that you don't care.
Yes, your children are just nicknames, photos, and anecdotes,
and maybe the shades of your voice and maybe your small sobs
that last morning as I woke up,
and then you went.
And then you went, and then
the valley revealed itself again,

and the fire crews dashed fervently about
and the helicopters rested, timing out at the airstrip
like matronly insects, and then they buzzed off.
And then all of your traces time-bombed in time together
and I found myself in the midst of a vast, unmappable space
and the map of the space was a gray blank and the legend
of the map had one symbol, a knitting needle,
and beside the symbol in the legend of the map
was your pretty name spelled out in black
like a place, like a fact.

SUCCESSION

Awake to an early thrush,
an elegant spider.

And anger telescoping ridgelines,
a federal lunch, a local harmonica.

A new tongue is cataloged
along with the trove of places,

property lines redrawn
by riverbanks migrating annually,

negative property lines,
an entire globe plus fifty yards, owned.

And a bonfire undersluiced by a river,
bagpiped by unwelcome wind,

lukewarm homebrew,
private items used inside the common room.

Six strings, eight notes, one year
and one night you binge on raucous light,

sky unknown, candles lighting
the softest skin

while the newly known ascends
to a treehouse built in evening's throat.

In the melt out, delta out, ablation zoning out
snow under the isolate sky,

the tiny fixity of a spore in gravel
where the first spider

legs out onto new rock,
dust fall glissade of willow cotton,

catkin singularities in green space,
a familiar but unknown birdcall,

the wind in leaves in terrible stereo,
ache of much sun on sweaty skin,

the insulation of knowing this,
wanting to know, discovering a crack

in a favorite cup lifted from its shelf
by a window, filling it anyhow with wine.

IN REVIEW

It seems I'm your letter, posted and returned,
also the sound of the key
sliding into your house
and then I make dinner.

Imagine all the fuss over
your garden beds
gone fallow, feral—
Farewell, kempt one, so long

your sequined dress was far away,
shinier than life,
the sequins were compact discs,
mixed, you named them

and charmed the brazen morning
and all around you your children,
yourself, art objects, décor.
Of course books, of course your pipe,

the fence, alarm system, the dainty oven,
of course the chance to barrel into one another,
in wind, in absence, enlisted here, together
are we insistent, may we or may we not suffice.

I foresee a skin of ice
slicking this intersection

where traffic signals choreograph
my departure, literal, tedious,
quiet, all color, light, bland, all breath,
held, held—

FIELD WORK

We have most of one year to measure loss,
that newcomer in our field of stones.

Which slow moisture wicks through your Mondays?
You monitor what gains on you with mirrors. At home

you watch the wreckage of so many meals
assembled on the counter. The young ones

offer their little explanations for the genius disaster
created with so many knots, saying "accident"

saying "just kidding." Soon it's time for a meal
and another, and another. For a year,

we measure time using months and weeks,
missing the earlier times made of days. We learn

that writhing things live in the field under the stones,
and that the stones once lived underwater.

We turn every stone as eagerly as if we would
sacrifice whatever we could find to the sun,

and the soil cakes itself under our fingernails
as if to remind us of something later,

at dinner, commas, parentheses, em dashes
standing by to help whatever words we mean to assemble.

AFTER THIS LIFE

The lisp of seasons we scarcely left
chime another morning haphazardly to light—
time to find myself in the woods, by the creek,
idealess, comfortless.
All lines line up or lift their sullen voices like winds.
If we could limit our house voice to mere thought
and sense all thoughts, if we could eat
or write our subarctic lives
without ever sounding churlish or devised—
I imagine first the changing leaves of trees
the morphing light of sunset striking slopes
where eager men careen up some false alpine
and nonplussed animals give up the idea of warmth.
You thought my life was lifted up by smoke.
We thought our lives could adopt elegant repetition.
And should you stay honest
between the first and last
of our thousand wedding days
I will hold a match before my mouth
and smoke the words *I do.*

ADDRESS FROM
A FAR-OFF HILL

Vocal chords are nothing like clothes or power lines.
This shelf of food is a month to drink
together in walls that membrane our wakings.

Delimit homespace, make trespass possible.
Admit our deserts are irrigated, decipher
hunger from crop names taunting interstate

from fence wire. Later horses almost all in fence.
Foothills sore and roaded,
unhinge, denounce the maddest quiet.

This valley will not absorb rain.
Maunder here, divagate from tongue-tied
reservations, whole fortnights blind-lined and day-striped.

Our mumbles, an effluence of decorum, unpicked apples
fermenting into yellow grass.
Quit the talk, go dark into the river,

dark when the water heaves you,
a glut of atmospheres, lick out
when nothing is left to swallow.

Make this the whistle-stop that ends travel
and build where the coin rusts to rail.

TRASH BURNING

I made your elegant fire
downriver under alpenglow.

You're newsworthy and obscure,
the last North American home,
and I roost in the eaves, a cliff swallow.

Ash, night, soot
marks your face, throat.

You are pent, I'm quiet
and we manage to compose
ourselves of gravel bar light.

I shovel embers haphazardly
into the river, burnt news

hiss of burnt paper plates
burnt maps of the backcountry
credit music.

More newsworthy than southern
experimental forests

you blossom
haphazard halfway
through summer.

THE SMALLEST ICE AGE

I barreled into your tempting weather.
I have it in me to be a weed in you.
I plummeted into the stillmost pools
and breathed water, I breathe water,
I am not shy to say I am thirsty,
you're the water, you are snow and I have thirst.
From the smallest ice age, I'm thirsty,
I am borne by ice toward you.
Are you stationary,
is this lake bed real?
Would you fingerpaint
the story for me using this pasty mud
made of glacier silt? There are places, high,
where every bird is a miracle.
Are you the updraft shepherding birds into heights,
are you the pollen of the flower's looking,
leaking color out where colors are as mineral as bodies,
where rockfall splashes brilliantly to lakes,
where the brain dribbles a river out
to other distant rivers—are we tied, here, are we affronted
by nothing, behind one another,
beside ourselves, surrounded, ourselves, here, by this?

INROAD

Some minds wellspring out of their own inroads.
Some inroads terminate with the mind's wellspring's alms,
skewing all speech-making thin, slipshod,
some blow glass versions of birdsongs they can't hear
while bear tracks downstream of the fish-weir
muddle rubber-booted biologists with mouths of numbers,
and the stream erodes the meanings under timber, under lumber.
River folk carve sonorous muteness from dried reeds
and store them inside mouths like wet beliefs.
Their talk is song and the songs get caught in trees
or settle there, ravens of the Pleiades.

ABLATION ZONE

You fluctuate snowlines
each morning migrating over
ridgelines on a tectonic plate
that moves as fast as
fingernails grow.

Each time wind
moves the willow's leaves
the mountain range uplifts—

Ice washes through a white slot canyon,
melts into gullets, maws,
grains of silt hesitate, it is glacier mud,
the world's smallest rock de-magnified.

You're a shade of aurora
and just as fleeting—
you inside beryl ice,
you within the abandoned vehicle,
terrarium growing every leafed succession,
you the painting
of ice melting around stones,
you the weather
that stacks up in layers when—

TRAVERSE

No stream by morning, a mountain-tap stopped.
And so no water, no sleep, no walls.
And now a long pack, in katabatic wind,
our throats' automatic knowledge
of how to place water inside.
We stuffed goat fur in our pockets
up high yesterday and descended toward
miles of moraines and white ice,
streambeds made of sky-colored ice
filled with ice gone liquid.
You say you'll spin this
white fur in our pockets.
Your bottle contains moments of this ice
we walk on while slowly changing
color in the sun, and your eyes,
carved by wind, by glaciers and mountains,
see snow melt into moulins
and crevasses, snow this ice muddies
as it gathers in surface-streams
and subsurface channels
disgorged as a river
miles down from here.
Silt lines the contours
of our hands, sweat salts our faces
in wind, and ice
warms in our bodies' cells.

THUMBNAIL SPRING SONG

Even now I do not believe it,
despite Weather slipping its wilted noose
of braided dandelion stems around Summer's throat
down on the lower hemline of the bank
which looks wet, and is.
That swollen creek was new when we arrived.
The weather around us explains
exactly what happens on the coast.
Inland, the ruins of white houses
all transformed actual acts of conversion
into mossy roofs and gaping windows, lost teeth.
A spider suspends itself in a glassless windowpane,
one dark kernel against a glinting wet distance
where a black bear swims from one island to another.
We thrill at its tracks as if our seeing them mattered.
Give me distancelessness, give humility.
Wait seventeen minutes and the
moon will show on the ridge.
Lie down but keep your eyes open to hear
evening translated through bird throats.
Hold ground but retreat into the watery calls,
thumbnail spring songs, make the river
a mantra. For now,
you have juncos and sparrows,
swallows and redpolls. The ravens notice you
there on the bank where the sun stained

the exposed skin of your neck and ears,
the skin of your perfect features. The sun
has grown this meal so eat,
eat, eat it, drink the water, stay home, here,
come home where the hot water
has its moments with the steeping leaves.

SKY BEHIND WEATHER

Are you just weather

and birds?
Always the light
forging colors from air,

curtains of rain

and some measure
of distance to peaks.
We see our former selves,

poorer, with bright lichen eyes

and time for the weathered core
of this old volcano, frost-wedged
and slid down into

a painting.   A symmetry develops

between the campfire and the aurora.
They are responsive, attentive,
and the water sings that out

the still lake sings that out.

The sky behind weather
is a forests' worth of berries
illuminating unseeable attics in birds.

Our selves behind sleep almost know us

almost consider leaving
a note on the table
in the window.

STEEPED

Outside the cabin, black rain
runs into a glass rainbow,
an actual one lighting
an actual willow bush
already turned yellow inside
the still-green forest.
I think I'll never leave
and in staying I will
drink a lifetime's worth
of the kind creek. I say
I'll meet you in town
in one month
and we'll eat dinner.
Two thousand miles
down the coast,
a black bear swims
to a beach on an island
capped with a house
and bites holes in a rubber
Zodiac that deflates
as the sun comes up.
The family, asleep inside,
is stranded, and the animal
is gone when they wake.

Inside my cabin,
I boil rainwater for tea
and listen to the birdless quiet
as leaves steep and slabs of color
bleed back into the wet light.

THE WILD DEAD

We discovered a variety of odd and small deaths
a mile out on the ice—
voledeath, hawkdeath, goatdeath
sudden smudges of color the sound of cold water
loud enough to shimmer the sky into quiet.
What melts curious precisions from ice?
A single-prop drones far off like an interstate.
I perceived the blister of your isolation
swell with unnatural animal fluid.
I watched you ascend your hallucination—
you preferred minutes spent starkly realizing.
Can I pare the pale glimmer of your shoulders
from my catalog of wants?
You are the form the sky is against.
Your arms bracket
small deaths, cubdeaths, avalanched and thawed.
Snow burial repealed a summer set on decomposition,
then autumn built itself
on the bones of unraveled bodies.

ACKNOWLEDGEMENTS

Thanks to the editors responsible for publishing earlier versions of many of these poems in the *Anchorage Daily News*, *Black Warrior Review*, *Colorado Review*, *Cirque*, *Left-Facing Bird*, *Ice Floe II*, and *LitSite Alaska*. An earlier version of the long poem "Fata Morgana" was published by Blue Hour Press as a digital chapbook.

Thanks to the staff and editors of University of Alaska Press and the Alaska Literary Series advisory board for their careful attention, especially James Engelhardt and Peggy Shumaker.

Deep thanks to the friends and teachers whose involvement, influence, or example have brought so much pleasure and purpose to the process: Dan Beachy-Quick, Bruce Beasley, Elizabeth Bradfield, Lucie Brock-Broido, Mike Burwell, Kaeli Casati, Elizabeth Chicken, Nancy Cook, Phil Condon, Olena Kalytiak Davis, Scott Dixon, Lucas Farrell, Gary Geddes, Sally Gibert, Michelle Glazer, Lee Gulyas, Kelsea Habecker, Brenda Hillman, Joan Naviyuk Kane, Nabil Kashyap, Mickey Kenny, Joanna Klink, Bill Knott, Alyse Knorr, Youna Kwak, Michael Lukas, Carmen Costas Malvar, Molly McDonald, Leif Mjos, Susanna J. Mishler, David Mitchell, Grace Ortman, Nancy Pagh, Greg Pape, Kate Partridge, D. A. Powell, Cathy Tagnak Rexford, Eva Saulitus, Peter Sennhauser, Ben Shaine, Brandon Shimoda, Jessie Sobey, Frank Soos, Jessica Speed, Heather Tone, Karen Volkman, and Alyssa Von Lehman Lopez. Thanks, too, to the 49 Writers community.

Love and gratitude to my families.